REIMAGINING DEMOCRACY

McCourtney Institute for Democracy

The Pennsylvania State University's McCourtney Institute for Democracy (http://democracyinstitute.la.psu.edu) was founded in 2012 as an interdisciplinary center for research, teaching, and outreach on democracy. The institute coordinates innovative programs and projects in collaboration with the Center for American Political Responsiveness and the Center for Democratic Deliberation.

Laurence and Lynne Brown Democracy Medal

The Laurence and Lynne Brown Democracy Medal recognizes outstanding individuals, groups, and organizations that produce exceptional innovations to further democracy in the United States or around the world. In even numbered years, the medal spotlights practical innovations, such as new institutions, laws, technologies, or movements that advance the cause of democracy. Awards given in odd numbered years highlight advances in democratic theory that enrich philosophical conceptions of democracy or empirical models of democratic behavior, institutions, or systems.

REIMAGINING DEMOCRACY

LESSONS IN DELIBERATIVE DEMOCRACY
FROM THE IRISH FRONT LINE

DAVID M. FARRELL AND
JANE SUITER

CORNELL SELECTS

an imprint of

CORNELL UNIVERSITY PRESS

Ithaca and London

Cornell Selects, *an imprint of Cornell University Press, provides a forum for advancing provocative ideas and fresh viewpoints through outstanding digital and print publications. Longer than an article and shorter than a book, titles published under this imprint explore a diverse range of topics in a clear and concise format—one designed to appeal to any reader. Cornell Selects publications continue the press's long tradition of supporting high quality scholarship and sharing it with the wider community, promoting a culture of broad inquiry that is a vital aspect of the mission of Cornell University.*

Open access edition funded by the McCourtney Institute for Democracy at Pennsylvania State University

First published 2019 by Cornell University Press

Library of Congress Cataloging-in-Publication Data

Library of Congress Control Number:2019908639

Contents

REIMAGINING DEMOCRACY

Introduction

On a wet Friday evening in June 2011, we were standing in the lobby of a hotel located in the suburbs of Dublin. Months of hard work traveling around the country promoting the idea of a "new Ireland" had led to this moment—the start of Ireland's first national citizens' assembly. In the previous weeks we and our colleagues had been working the phones, talking with the 150 citizens who had been selected randomly by a market research company. The venue for the Citizens' Assembly was ready to go; our trained facilitators were in the hotel bar making last moment preparations; the media had been notified to turn up the next day. This was the key moment for our "We the Citizens" project. We were as ready as we could possibly be—the anxious question in our heads was whether our citizens would show up on a wet night. The fact that our Citizens' Assembly weekend coincided with a Neil Diamond concert hadn't helped. Hotel rooms across Dublin were as rare as hen's teeth that weekend, which was why we ended up using a hotel and location that were not, by any stretch of the imagination, our first choice. Gradually, people started arriving—in ones, and twos, and then larger numbers. They were made up of a diverse mix of young and old, a few students, quite a few who had never been to university, a couple of farmers, one elderly gent with a smile on his face that never seemed to fade—people from the four corners of Ireland. We counted them in, ensured they had a drink, and prayed they'd stay. In the end one hundred showed up—two thirds of our target figure, but just enough to allow us to proceed. Any fewer and we would have been in difficulty.

Background

The images of Ireland adorning the pages of the world's newspapers in recent years have been of a progressive, tolerant country: young people celebrating liberal referendum victories, waving rainbow flags in the front courtyard of Dublin Castle. Those watching these referendums—whether conservative or liberal, disappointed or euphoric—were aware that these crowds portrayed a fundamental shift in values. Ireland was becoming a most unlikely poster child of progressive values. Division that had long haunted a society based largely on a strict interpretation of the Catholic Church's values were being swept away. In an extraordinarily short time, Ireland was transforming itself, embracing values unthinkable only a decade earlier. So, what had happened? Can Ireland's experience provide any lessons for other countries seeking change, a reduction in polarization, and a healing of divisions?

Our story can begin in any number of places—in the drafting of the conservative Catholic constitution in 1937, in the years of austere social values, in the abuse scandals which emerged in the 1990s and 2000s, and, crucially, in the crisis following the "Great Recession" of 2008.[1] After all, crisis is often a great innovator. As Churchill remarked, "Never let a good crisis go to waste." The steps that Ireland took amid the heat of that crisis—seeking to build trust, listen to the people, and engage in open and constructive dialogue—provided the impetus for change. Perhaps parts our story will even sound familiar to readers elsewhere in the world.

In 2009, Ireland was in the midst of an existential crisis: a severe recession was combined with a series of bank failures and the arrival of the "troika" (the International Monetary Fund, European Union, and European Central Bank) to bail out the country under strict terms and conditions. Unemployment increased rapidly, more than doubling from 6.5 percent in July 2008 to 14.8 percent in July 2012, despite renewed waves of emigration. Demonstrators flooded the

Dublin streets, though unlike in Athens and elsewhere where the troika had had to intervene, Ireland's protests remained mostly nonviolent.[2] Unsurprisingly, an *Irish Times* MRBI poll found that public trust in the government had fallen to 10 percent—almost the lowest of the twenty-nine countries in the EU, with only Hungary, Latvia, Lithuania, and Greece returning lower degrees of trust. Only a year earlier, that number was 46 percent, when Ireland was still enjoying unparalleled economic wealth during its era as the "Celtic Tiger."

Seeing their economic circumstances collapse and feeling the pinch of austerity measures, the public pointed the finger of blame at the government. Political cynicism was rife. When the beleaguered government had finally run its course, the public voted them out of office; the 2011 general election was the most dramatic election result in the history of the state.[3] An opinion poll survey commissioned by the main Irish broadcaster (RTÉ) sought to understand the main reasons citizens voted the way they did. In large part, those reasons boiled down to a feeling of being let down by politics and politicians.

Of course, declining trust in institutions and in politics is not unique to Ireland, nor to countries exercising severe recession.[4] Declining levels of trust represent a danger to democracy. Indeed, we live in a time when democracy itself seems under siege. This was the point made by the late, highly respected Irish political scientist Peter Mair in his posthumous *Ruling the Void*.[5] The indicators are familiar enough: Fewer of us are bothering to vote in elections. Among those who do vote, there are dramatic shifts from one party to another and increasingly from the moderate ranks to the extreme fringes. Demagogic political candidates are at the fore, and where these demagogues win power, they seem determined to dismantle the fabric of our democratic institutions. In its moment of great economic jeopardy, Ireland was in grave danger of following this dismal path. Our view was that something needed to be done to reduce these risks, or to at least to mitigate their worst affects. This is the story of what we sought to do and what was achieved.

Part I

The Irish Front Line

Clearing the Path for a Nationwide Mini-Public

As early as 2009, members of the political science department-ments of Irish universities, including ourselves, had set up a working group under the aegis of the Political Studies Association of Ireland. Our primary mission was to respond to the ongoing crisis and to the increasingly vocal debate over the need for changes to the political system and wider public life. The group—of no uniform ideological bent—did not always agree on the nature of reforms needed, but we all agreed on the importance of informed debate.

The group implemented a series of initiatives involving various teams of political scientists who worked together with a broader set of colleagues. In the years that followed, the resulting Irish Citizens Assembly project was involved with three key events: a 2011 experimental and pilot study known as "We the Citizens," the 2012–2014 Convention on the Constitution, and the 2016–2018 Irish Citizens Assembly—each building on previous successes.

Our first steps on this long journey were twofold: (1) we focused on promoting the kinds of systemic political reform that would increase the government's responsiveness, openness, and accountability, and (2) we set out a process designed to increase the opportunities for regular people to be listened to.

The first approach was aimed at supercharging the political reform debate in the February 2011 election. It was one thing to have the entire country griping about the government, but it was another to get people talking about pragmatic improvements. Our goals depended not only on the political science community but also on activists, web designers, and data analysts because our efforts relied heavily on op-eds and online measures. One of these was the relaunching of a blog (Politicalreform.ie) dedicated to examining specific policy failures and offering solutions. Another site important in the heat of the 2011 general elections was Reformcard.com, an online measurement tool that ranked each party based on the quality of their proposals for political reform. Reformcard.com provided twenty-five proposals for political forum aimed at transforming the political system and making it fit for the twenty-first century. We judged each party's reform policies in five broad areas of the political system—legislative, electoral, open government, local government, and public services—using five indicators for each area. In total, each party was scored on twenty-five aspects of political reform and was graded out of a maximum of one hundred for the effectiveness of their proposals. This was a tool designed to help voters decide, but extensive media coverage demanded that the parties take it seriously. As a result, every party included an extensive section on political reform within their 2011 election manifestos.

The second initiative focused on the process of reform, on proposing bottom-up, citizen-oriented approaches centered on the use of deliberative forums. Along with colleagues Elaine Byrne and Eoin O'Malley, we submitted a proposal to Atlantic Philanthropies for a project relating to deliberative democracy that would be transparent, independent, and objective. We proposed to call it We the Citizens. We the Citizens was organized with the support of the Irish Universities Association, the representative body for the seven Irish universities. The idea behind this deliberative approach was the professional and personal conviction that it could help citizens recapture trust in their political process. Through it, citizens could join the decision-making process—not as elected officials, but simply as engaged, everyday voters—and act as a bridge between the people and their politicians, reconciling a democratic deficit that had been feeding so much bitterness.

Our group had seen promising results in other countries around the world. For instance, Canada had used citizens assemblies to deliberate on reforming the electoral systems in British Columbia (2004) and Ontario (2007), as had the Netherlands (2006).[6] And, of course, these citizens' assemblies were just one form of a "deliberative mini-public"; others have included the citizens' juries that originated in the US in the 1970s, the Danish consensus conferences that date from the 1980s, German planning cells that date from the 1970s, or James Fishkin's deliberative polls that originated in the 1990s.[7] All share the use of small groups of randomly selected citizens, operating according to deliberative principles (including facilitated small-group discussions) and tasked with considering one or a number of important policy, institutional, or constitutional reform issues. The citizens' assemblies are generally seen as the superior form of a deliberative mini-public because they are large (generally including one hundred or more citizens), operate over a long period (thus allowing time for more detailed discussions), and their outcomes lead to referendums involving the wider body of citizens in a nation-state.

In other words, political scientists like us already knew the benefits: assemblies involve rational, reasoned discussion with a cross-section of an entire population, and they use various methods of inquiry such as directly questioning experts. The process is not adversarial, although disagreement is inevitable and valued because it allows space for an inclusive process of dialogue and discussion. It promotes creativity and tends to build consensus rather than separating people into winning and losing sides—but there is no requirement of unanimity. Deliberative processes are not meant to replace representative or direct democracy, but to enhance and support it. We were hopeful, and indeed, the ideal held some appeal with the general public.

Of course, such a proposal also had many detractors. Some argued that "we already have a citizens' assembly; it's called the parliament!" Others wondered aloud about the abilities of "ordinary citizens" to have the capacity or the time to deal with complicated topics—the implication being that politics is too complicated for the average citizen and that matters of importance are better left in the hands of professional politicians. We profoundly disagreed with both charges.

At its heart, We the Citizens was a research project designed to test these worries and to establish whether more deliberative mechanisms for citizen involvement would have a positive effect on democracy. We the Citizens was a two-phased project designed to add impetus to these commitments. For the first phase, we held a series of public meetings in seven different locations around the country. These provided an opportunity for people to share ideas and concerns that could feed into the eventual national Citizens' Assembly. They also served as awareness-raising exercises in cities and towns around the country, supporting our first initiative of raising public awareness of the possibility for greater citizen involvement in our country's democracy.[8] Discussion reinforced that while this was the worst economic recession in Irish history, it was not the first. The diagnosis was a malfunctioning political system: criticisms pointed out that it was mired in the pork barrel, lacked accountability, and was run by politicians distant from the people. What was most revealing from these public meetings was a sheer hunger for reflective dialogue. Our worries about these meetings running out of control proved unfounded. What became quickly apparent was that people were prepared to park their anger at the door and enter the room to talk, not fight.

In the meantime, the country elected new leaders in February 2011. The two main political parties which formed the resulting Irish government committed to various forms of citizen or constitutional assemblies in their election manifestos—thanks, in part, to our activities during that campaign to promote discussion of bottom-up approaches to political reform. The parties that formed a new government after that election promised to establish a "constitutional convention" that would include citizens as members, but they were vague on the details. The principal mission of We the Citizens, therefore, was to help guide the government on how to do this, ensuring that the parties fulfilled their campaign promises.

The second phase of We the Citizens was about forming, at last, the Citizens' Assembly. Crucially, it would be the pilot program for others to come.

Anatomy of a First Assembly

At the heart of our project—in 2011 and today—is the idea that politicians must be prepared to listen to the people, to believe that the people can be trusted with decisions, to weigh up evidence, and to come to conclusions that are in society's best interest. Basic enough, right? In the traditional understanding of representative democracy, the people would simply elect politicians to represent their interest: they had the opportunity to "kick the rascals out." But in an increasingly fragmented and globalized world, this model is under strain: voters feel increasingly detached and national governments appear less in control of events. This often leads to a gap between the elites and the people, a gap which can then be harnessed by populist and other actors seeking to exploit human vulnerably when trust is in decline.

What Is Deliberative Democracy?

Academic definition: Deliberative democracy can be defined as "a process of reaching reasoned agreement among free and equal citizens, ensuring that they have an opportunity to express their views and preferences and justify their decisions within a deliberative process for the purpose of reaching conclusions that are collectively binding."[9]

We can trace the roots of deliberative democracy back to Aristotle and Ancient Greece, where all citizens in the *demos* came together in the public square to debate and to decide on the issues of the day. The German philosopher Jurgen Habermas—and indeed many others—have refined it and there are variations in interpretation. What is common to all conceptions is that those involved must deliberate, based on evidence, before voting. Thus the debate should be informed and balanced by evidence from all sides of an argument; it should be civil and repetitive, such that all points of view held by significant portions of the population should be repeated for all to hear.

For us, a citizens' assembly offers a means to reduce the risks to that traditional, democratic model. The simple idea is to bolster representative democracy through adding a deliberative element: a forum where people of different persuasions can come together to listen to one another. The goal is to become informed, understand, and to come to conclusions—in essence combining deliberative with representative democracy in order to strengthen democracy overall.

With all this in mind, our first assembly in 2011 relied on a randomly selected cross section of Irish society. This randomness was important. That rainy June weekend, the group who turned up at a South Dublin hotel to deliberate included students and the curious, young and old, men and women, but mainly those taken from a group of 1,242 people randomly polled. Members had not attended the regional events and were not representing any area or group. The only selection criterion, other than that they be part of the original survey group, was that the overall group be as representative as possible of the Irish population. While nobody was asked to state their occupation, it was evident that the mix of people who attended included employers, the unemployed, public and private sector workers, students, small-businesspeople, and also people who worked in the home. The ages ranged from approximately fifteen to eighty. Among them was one older lady who had never voted in her life and was thrilled that someone wanted her opinion.

Our hotel and the weather may not have been ideal, but it turned out that the location for the Citizens' Assembly the next day was perfect. We convened in Dublin's city center at the Great Hall of the Royal Hospital Kilmainham, a beautifully restored seventeenth-century structure whose grandeur invoked something of our lofty hopes for the project. The Citizens' Assembly members were bussed in from the hotel (a job in itself to round up everyone on time). On arrival, and after a short interlude for a group photograph, members were seated at round tables of eight, each having a facilitator and notetaker, with paper tablecloths and markers to give everyone an opportunity to write down their own unmediated thoughts and comments. The meeting started with a short video that had been produced overnight by the project's cameraman. Unknown to us he had approached each member as they arrived in the hotel and got their permission to take a few photos, splicing them together to produce a short but wonderful video that served beautifully to introduce the members to each other. The reaction was electric: no one in the room could be in any doubt that they were at the start of an important moment, and furthermore, that their presence was valued.

The agenda was set on the basis of the issues raised in the regional events that had been held around the country in May and early June 2011. Over the next two days, the members were asked to deliberate on a number of political reform questions relating to representation and on divisive topics of interest to Irish citizens at the time—the appropriate balance between taxation and spending, property taxes, water charges, sale of state assets, and student fees.

The session started with a brief presentation by one or more experts, summarizing the key arguments that were set out in the briefing documents circulated the evening before. The purpose of the briefing documents and the expert panel was to provide the participants with the background information they needed to have an informed discussion.

Next, they were given an opportunity to deliberate among themselves, with the experts available to answer questions of detail or fact. This was followed by a plenary session in which all members were invited to comment on their initial sets of recommendations—this was done via roaming mikes.

In most cases, the tables nominated a spokesperson to share the table's recommendations with the assembly, though there were also individual contributions. Initially, the reticence to speak up was evident, but as the day progressed and members grew in confidence, the problem became one of how to keep to time.

The Citizens' Assembly members were then given another opportunity to deliberate in small groups to finalize and word their recommendations; in all instances, each table was dealing with the same issue simultaneously. As the session drew to a close, they were asked to propose recommendations about the issue at hand and these were gathered in for each table. Once the recommendations had been collated, a ballot paper was produced and the Citizens' Assembly members were given an opportunity to vote on their recommendations.

Inevitably, the agenda item that proved most difficult to come to a resolution on was the economy—the final matter discussed on Sunday morning. Emotions ran high, at least in some of the tables. As one member commented afterwards: "One of the issues that came up on our table is that we feel there's an elephant in the room here, and that is the debts that we owe the banks and the fact that a bank like Anglo Irish—a speculative investment bank—was underwritten by the state. And we're talking about a third of national debt has gone to pay off these debts which should not be the responsibility of the Irish citizens, and I feel that this is one of the biggest issues facing the country right now." Views were so strong on this agenda item—not surprising given the dire state of the Irish economy at the time—that it resulted in a large ballot paper with more than one hundred recommendations. It is important to note, however, that at this pilot assembly, the voting was not a core element of the scientific process. The We the Citizens team chose to add in a ballot at the end of each session to give the participants in the pilot assembly some sense of completing a process. In a real citizens' assembly (such as the two Irish processes that followed), the recommendations would be sent back time and time again to the participants for further deliberation and refining.

Ultimately, the general tone of the debates was constructive, with participants listening to each other's views and giving one another the opportunity to speak, even when their views were very different. The groups made good use of the experts, asking them to clarify specific points and to provide international or best-practice examples when, for instance, there was a disagreement on which the group was stuck. As one would expect, some groups were more talkative than others. There were a small number of instances where a very strong personality dominated the discussion, though generally this tended not to happen, as the facilitators were able to manage the dynamic and keep some balance in terms of contribution within the groups. In general, people were satisfied with the agenda and how the discussions were moderated.

The value of our pilot Citizens' Assembly held in June 2011 cannot be overestimated. The concerns we had on that rainy night at the start of the weekend were wiped away: one hundred citizens had turned up and stayed the course. They listened to the experts, engaged in respectful and informed dialogue, and formed clear conclusions about the matters they had discussed. And crucially for our purposes, our surveys of them produced the sorts of findings that we had expected to find. The survey data demonstrated that when compared to their starting position (i.e., before their involvement in the Citizens' Assembly) and also when compared with a sample of citizens who had not participated in the process, our participants showed greater interest in politics, and they become more willing to discuss and become more involved in politics going forward.[10]

Encouragingly, at the end of the process, our participants also felt more positive about the ability of ordinary people to influence politics. We observed large shifts in the opinions of Citizens' Assembly members after they had deliberated on economic issues such as taxation, spending, and the sale of state assets. These opinion shifts were statistically significant and distinctly different from those of the various control groups that were built into the political science experiment that was at the heart of the We the Citizens project. In other words, we emerged confident that the changes we observed were not random or a result of chance: it was the participation in the Citizens' Assembly that had caused these positive changes. In short, we had clear, formidable evidence that participation in a citizens' assembly produces better-informed and more satisfied citizens—in Ireland and (as existing research shows) elsewhere, too.

Reception

A single assembly, of course, is not enough to influence one nation's public sentiment, let alone change the world. A week after our first event concluded, a special program ran in the primetime evening slot on the national broadcaster, RTÉ. This program was the result of intense prior discussions we had with senior RTÉ executives when we launched our We the Citizens project; we'd built in a budget line item to bring a large portion of our Citizens' Assembly members back to Dublin for this live program. The voices of these randomly selected citizens were overwhelmingly in favor of the process—but, at least initially, we were met with a cynical response from many journalists and politicians.

Prime-Time Special on the Citizens' Assembly, RTÉ Television, July 4, 2011

"I know I had the vote, but I didn't feel that I had a voice."
—Annette Ferguson, Blackrock, County Louth

"I'm just a Regular-John Citizen, but like multiples of thousands of John and Joan Citizens over the last decade and a half, I have become very disillusioned with the disconnect that has developed between the body politic and the people who are there that are meant to represent us. So when I found the opportunity to join the Citizens' Assembly, I said to myself that it is better to light one candle than curse the darkness. It may or may not prove to be influential in the end, but it is better to do something than nothing at all, and I think that this organization could be a very useful adjunct to the status-quo body politic in this country. If they listen to us, perhaps we can fill the middle ground between the top and the bottom, which is very, very badly needed."

—P. J. Walsh, Ballymahon, County Longford

"I think it is very important to have elected people make the executive decisions, but I felt the [Citizens' Assembly] was a very good way of listening to the ordinary people—not people who have set up blogs or are in pressure groups. One thing that we found was that what everybody wanted was for politicians to sort out the system, not somebody's medical card."

—Tom Cavanagh, Shankill, County Dublin

Yet we, like the assembly members, were optimistic. The experiment had demonstrated that Irish people, even those randomly selected, could be trusted to deliberate, to come to views based on evidence, and to trust one another and the system more. The resulting report was presented to the leaders of every political party in Ireland in a series of bilateral meetings. Examining the report, senior politicians could see that this was indeed a possible way forward to rebuild trust. Some still expressed a degree of skepticism about the scope or full potential of an initiative like this in "the real world," but most expressed at least a willingness to give it a go—and particularly so for the leaders of the two parties in government.

As a result, in November of that same year, the Convention on the Constitution was announced. It was to consider a wide range of measures (reviewed below) and to include both regular citizens and politicians. The time for real citizen participation in Ireland had begun.

The Citizens' Assembly project now moved to its next phase—supporting the work of a real-world deliberative mini-public. But these were still nervous times for us. Standing in the rain on that wet Friday night, we'd worried about whether our weekend-long experiment would work. Now that the process was being taken up by government to be launched on a grand scale, our worry was whether it would go to plan: Would all the political parties cooperate? Would the civil servants put in charge of running the process keep to the "deliberative democracy" script? Would the citizens engage and stay the course? Would the media provide fair (or indeed, any) coverage? Would the process produce reasonable and credible outcomes? And what would happen to those outcomes once the process had completed its work?

We the Citizens had been created to make substantive changes in the nation's political process. The next chapter, then, involves the 2012–2014 Convention on the Constitution—which built on the success and new credibility of our pilot Citizens' Assembly, but in this instance, its mission was to discuss the foundational document of our republic. As we shall see below, this convention was responsible for the progressive reforms unveiled to the world a few years later, and also showcased another method of forming such an assembly—a hybrid composed of both citizens and politicians.

A Hybrid Model: Citizens and Politicians

In late 2012, the Irish government established the Convention on the Constitution, which followed many of the organizational features and procedures spearheaded by We the Citizens. Specifically, it once again included randomly selected citizen members and followed carefully facilitated and informed small-group discussions. It met for fourteen months between December 2012 and February 2014.

One clear difference with the We the Citizens process was that the membership of the convention comprised sixty-six citizens selected randomly from the greater population by

a market research company but also thirty-three legisla-
tors from the Irish parliament nominated by their respec-
tive parties, including representatives from the political
parties in the Northern Ireland Assembly. The hundredth
member was the chair, Tom Arnold, a respected individual
from the charity sector.[11] We formed the core of the Academic and Legal Support Group for the Convention; joining
us were two other political scientists—Eoin O'Malley (who
had worked with us on the We the Citizens project) and
Clodagh Harris—and a practicing lawyer, Lia O'Hegarty.[12]
The secretariat reserved space for a series of weekends in
a seaside hotel near Dublin, one with very good Wi-Fi, for
deliberation.

Onlookers were wary of the politicians' involvement.
After all, politicians are professional communicators and are,
on average, better educated than the average citizen. There
were prominent journalists who penned op-eds expressing
concerns that the politicians might dominate the discussion
and deliberations. We will address this in more detail in just
a moment, but suffice to say here, the organizers (ourselves
included) shared this concern and measures were taken to
prevent it, not least of all through the use of trained facilitators to ensure that all members had an equal voice in discussions. In addition, the chair established a set of principles
by which the convention should operate, and he repeatedly
reminded members of these principles and included them
in his introduction to each of the reports. The key mantras

were (1) openness and transparency (2) fairness (3) equality of voice, and (4) collegiality.[13]

In the lead-up to the opening meeting, political, academic, and media circles expressed skepticism about the convention. Some critics judged its agenda as too narrow. Others questioned whether the proposed model of deliberative democracy, involving randomly selected citizens and politicians, would even work. In addition, people doubted whether the government would take the exercise seriously, notwithstanding a commitment to provide a response to each recommendation within four months and set a time frame for recommendations that should go to referendum. As we shall see, in most respects, these criticisms proved unfounded.

The convention was tasked by the government with considering some eight topics:

- the term of the Irish presidency;
- whether to reduce the voting age for citizens;
- electoral reform;
- the right for citizens outside the state to vote in presidential elections;
- marriage equality;
- the role of women in the constitution;
- the participation of women in politics and public life; and
- blasphemy.

In addition, the convention added a few more items to its agenda: parliamentary reform and whether to insert a clause on economic, social, and cultural rights into our constitution. It's worth pausing a moment to appreciate the breadth and progressivism of some of these issues—not just in Ireland but in other countries around the world. Regular Irish citizens were being entrusted with deliberating on key issues such as marriage equality, the role of women, and voting rights.

The convention met over ten weekends for day-and-a-half sessions; arriving on Friday evening and departing by lunchtime on Sunday. Each meeting had three components: (1) presentation by experts of papers that had been circulated in advance; (2) debate between groups advocating on either side of an issue; and (3) roundtable discussions involving facilitators and notetakers. On Sunday morning, the members considered again the discussions of the previous day and voted on a ballot paper that reflected the details of the debate.

A good example of how this process operated is the weekend-long discussion on marriage equality in April 2013. The courts' interpretation of the Irish constitution was that it prevented the state from legislating for full gay marriage. The convention, therefore, was asked to consider the question of whether there should be a referendum to change the constitution to allow for marriage equality. The convention members received expert testimony (including documentation circulated in advance) from senior and respected constitutional lawyers (or "senior counsel"), academic lawyers, and child psychologists. There were also presentations by advocates on either side of the argument—included in the mix were a Catholic bishop and the children of same-sex couples.

The discussion of this topic included some truly memorable moments, such as toward the end of the weekend when one of the citizen members, who had not spoken before, stood up to make a personal statement. He spoke clearly but with some emotion: it was obvious to all in the room that he wanted to make a strong point. A kind of electric potential charged the air as everyone seemed to sense the nature of what he was about to say. He had been abused as a small child, he said, and the experience had affected his attitudes toward gay people. Here, in this room, he felt it was important to declare his view: he had no problem at all with the proposal for gay marriage. The hair rose on the backs of our necks. Applause broke out. Members rose to their feet, clapping.

The room was full throughout the weekend with journalists and other observers; although all of these were present only for the plenary discussion and were asked to leave while the small roundtable discussions were underway. Indeed, there were more people than could be accommodated in the room, and as a result, an overflow room had to be arranged with live streaming. The topic #marref trended on Twitter throughout the weekend.

After two days of intense discussion, the recommendation was clear: the members voted by an overwhelming majority

(79 percent in favor) that there should be a referendum on marriage equality. In addition, they voted (again by a large majority) in favor of legislation to clarify the issues of parentage, guardianship, and the upbringing of children by same-sex couples.

The reaction to the vote was immediate and loud. Cheering could be heard from the corridors outside the room, and there followed a night of celebrating in the gay bars across Ireland. This was seen as a seminal moment in the long campaign for gay rights in Ireland and internationally.[14] It is generally accepted that it finally persuaded an otherwise socially conservative prime minister to accept and embrace the call for marriage equality to the extent that he went on to play a prominent role in the referendum campaign that followed. Marriage equality was approved at a referendum on May 22, 2015, by 62 percent of voters on a turnout of 61 percent. Thus, Ireland became the first country in the world to approve marriage equality through a people's vote rather than by court decision or parliamentary (or congressional) act.

In total, the convention made forty-three recommendations, eighteen of which would require constitutional amendment by a referendum. To date, there have been three such referenda, two successful (on marriage equality in 2015 and blasphemy in 2018) and one not (on reducing the age requirement of presidential candidates). There have also been extensive parliamentary reforms, and further reforms are promised or are still being considered.

The fact that the convention catalyzed such important changes—especially the hugely successful referendum on marriage equality—makes Ireland a world first. The previous real-world examples of deliberation on a larger scale (the citizens' assemblies of British Columbia, Ontario, and the Netherlands) proved unsuccessful in terms of policy outcomes. One major reason for this was a disconnect between the citizen members and the wider political class who were excluded from the deliberative process and who therefore neither paid much heed to it nor supported its outcomes. In fact, some felt that a factor behind the success of the Irish assembly was its mixed membership, sixty-six randomly selected citizens working side by-side with thirty-three professional politicians, with the latter anchoring the process in the political system, making it more likely that the convention's recommendations would receive a fair hearing. One question, then, is whether politicians undermined the mini-public design of the convention by overwhelming the voices of ordinary citizens, at a cost to the deliberative process. However, in the detailed research that we have been able to carry out—based on extensive survey data gathered from the convention members—we find no evidence that politicians dominated the discussions. There is evidence of a slight liberal bias among the politician membership, but this had little effect on the outcomes.[15]

The lessons for the Irish political class were clear. A well-run citizens' assembly or convention can deliver a balanced, informed debate.

Breaking Conservative Orthodoxies: A Third Way

A third model for Ireland's democratic mini-publics is centered on a major plank of social and moral policy that had long needed a resolution: Ireland's constitutional ban on abortion. This is the issue that bedeviled successive Irish governments ever since the early 1980s, when a referendum was passed (in 1983) to insert an abortion ban into the constitution. The prevailing Catholic-oriented orthodoxies ensured that little could be done to resolve the issue. The success of the 2015 marriage equality referendum showed the potential of deliberative democracy to help ease the way for resolving difficult and emotive issues. Could it also help solve the decades-long problem of Ireland's abortion ban?

In the run-up to the 2016 election, pressure was mounting on politicians to tackle Ireland's abortion laws. Yet, the prevailing conservative orthodoxy was still present despite opinion polling that indicated strong support to remove the constitutional ban on abortion. By 2013, some 68 percent of voters were in favor of a referendum to make an exception for cases of rape or where the fetus will not be born alive, according to MRBI polls in *The Irish Times*. The death of a young mother was heavily publicized, and the UN Human Rights Committee found that Ireland's law prohibiting and criminalizing abortion violated women's human rights.

Yet, the issue was so polarizing and campaigners so vitriolic that politicians balked at taking action. Therefore, the outgoing government in 2015 proposed putting this divisive issue to the people in a citizens' assembly. The final push arrived when an independent (i.e., non-party) legislator in the parliament made it a condition of her joining the coalition government in 2016.

The assembly was mandated to look not only at abortion, but at climate change, fixed-term parliaments, and the "the manner in which referenda are held" (i.e., should we hold "super-referendum days," whereby a significant number of referenda are voted on in the same day). Nevertheless, all eyes were focused on abortion.

This was the first topic that the assembly dealt with. Their work covered a five-month period from late 2016 and included five meetings and plenty of reading material to wade through. As in the previous process, the members heard from a mix of experts—constitutional lawyers, healthcare practitioners, and ethicists—and campaigners advocating for each side of the issue. They also heard harrowing personal testimonies from women who either had an abortion or who decided not to.

A secret-ballot vote was held at the end of the process with the members voting overwhelmingly to replace the article with a new provision explicitly authorizing the Irish parliament to legislate for abortion and, of great surprise to watching pundits, for a very substantial liberalization of the abortion provision. Indeed, the degree of liberalization proposed attracted considerable journalistic comment. As one journalist remarked: "The results were more liberal than most would have imagined likely."[16] Another referred to the vote as a "landmark call."[17] An editorial in *The Irish Times* praised the Citizens' Assembly for performing "an important service in setting out a bold agenda for reform of our abortion laws."[18]

The assembly report was submitted to the Irish parliament, which convened a special committee to consider it in detail. That committee in turn recommended a referendum and legislation to liberalize Ireland's abortion rules, a move then endorsed by the parliament. The referendum was held on May 25, 2018 with a near-record turnout of 64 percent. The electorate voted to repeal the 8th Amendment by a majority of 66 percent to 34 percent, a result noted for its similarity to that of the Citizens' Assembly vote.[19]

It's worth underscoring that the Citizens' Assembly was composed solely of ordinary citizens; politicians were not involved due to the divisiveness of the topic. However, parliament was invested in the assembly: recall that parliament chose to convene it in the first place, and after the assembly delivered its report, a special parliamentary committee was waiting to discuss the report and its recommendations. Thus, a direct line still connected the assembly and the larger political system. As the convention had shown, this line matters— if politicians are involved in a process, they're more likely to feel invested in it, and thereby respect their responsibility to bring the assembly's work to a public vote.

As we have seen, the Citizens' Assembly followed in the wake of an earlier deliberative mini-public, the Constitutional Convention. And like its predecessor, it represented an important stage in the process leading up to the calling of a national referendum and also in its successful passage. Ireland, therefore, not only stands out internationally as the first country in the world to hold two constitutional mini-publics in quick succession, but also as a world leader in the linking of deliberative democracy (mini-publics) and direct democracy (referenda).

This speaks to a wider debate in the academic literature about how deliberation may not occur in isolation, but rather as part of the wider political system.[20] How this might operate in practice is still being discussed, but the Irish case suggests one route whereby a citizens' assembly helps inform a wider debate in society that leads to a national referendum about an important constitutional reform. In this way, citizens' assemblies can perform a discursive role, bringing the focus of referendum debates onto arguments that have been deliberatively scrutinized.

The 2016–2018 Irish Citizens' Assembly, like the Irish Convention on the Constitution before it, provides an instance of how deliberation can be inserted into the referendum process in a meaningful way. They illustrate powerful real-world examples of the potential "systemization" of deliberation.

Conclusion of Part I: Global Successes and Other Models

Deliberation and mini-publics are gaining currency beyond Ireland. Some of the resulting changes we've shown so far are specific to our country—for example, the inclusion of marriage equality and abortion within the constitution. But the value of the process, as we will show, is that facilitated mini-public debates bring people together during a time when political rhetoric is otherwise trying to tear them apart.

The assemblies in Ireland variously tackled topics as diverse as aging, climate change, and electoral reform. They brought people to at least a shared understanding of the problem, even if their solutions remain different. And as we've seen in this section, the forms of deliberative democracy have varied even across Ireland's recent attempts, each with their unique successes. Additionally, we can expand our survey to see even more examples of deliberative democracy tackling previously intractable issues. Nations and cities around the world—from Latin America to Europe and Africa—are seeking to embed deliberative democracy within their political systems. Here are some examples:

- **The Brexit debate in the United Kingdom.** The Citizens' Assembly on Brexit was held over two weekends in September 2017. It brought together fifty randomly selected citizens who reflected the diversity of the UK electorate. This was an opportunity for a diverse group of voters with differing viewpoints to learn about the issues of trade and migration from a variety of experts and politicians, deliberate with one another, and come to recommendations on the form that Brexit should take. The assembly was organized by an independent group of academics and civil society organizations. It revealed a much more nuanced picture of public opinion than many had come to expect. "Remainers" and "Leavers" engaged in detailed, reflective, and informed discussions about what the UK's post-Brexit relations with the European Union should be. Their discourse provided evidence that despite chaos at the Houses of Parliament in Westminster, citizens are willing and able to learn about, deliberate over, and come to subtle and well-considered recommendations on highly complicated and controversial policy issues. Although various leading politicians talked up the "no deal" option and stressed the overriding importance of strong control over immigration—the citizens' assembly arrived at a set of recommendations that ran counter to those position. To date, the British government has not accepted the calls for a government-sponsored citizens' assembly, but there are growing calls from politicians across all parties, and (at this writing) it cannot be ruled out in the future. If citizens can do this on an issue as divisive as Brexit, we strongly believe that citizens' assemblies and other deliberative processes can be used on a range of challenging political and constitutional issues.

- **The German-speaking parliament of East Belgium.** The "Ostbelgien Model" is a permanent and institutionalized citizen council set up by the government and parliament of the German-speaking region of Belgium. In 2018 and 2019, the Belgian G1000 convened a group of experts (including one of us) to help design a model for citizen participation in policy making. The mandate was to include the types of features we've discussed here: deliberative processes and random selection. Starting in September 2019, a fixed citizen council will set the agenda for one to three citizens' assemblies every year. These assemblies will come up with recommendations for regional policy, and parliament is required to respond.
- **France.** Le Grand Débat National was announced by the French president Emmanuel Macron as a response to the Yellow Vests movement and was launched in January 2019. It centered around four themes: ecological transition, taxation, organization of the state, and democracy and citizenship. It was made up a combination of regional meetings of self-selected groups in town halls often hosted by local mayors or even individual citizens. In addition, there were multiple opportunities to submit ideas—through mobile desks in train stations, for example, as well as online. Finally, there were randomly selected citizen assemblies in each of the French regions and five

overseas territories. It is still too early to tell what the result will be, and most reforms will require parliamentary approval or trade-offs.

- **Madrid, Spain.** Observatorio de la Ciudad, run by ParticipaLab, is an institutionalized body composed of forty-nine randomly selected participants. They rotate every year after eight sessions of work. Their main task is to review proposals coming from the popular civic-engagement website, Decide Madrid. They write a short report for every proposal before sending it to the public in the form of a referendum. They work under a deliberative dynamic with facilitation. This is a project from the city council, but ParticipaLab has been helping to inspire, design, and calibrate every detail. The Observatorio was preceded by the G1000 Madrid.

- **Toronto, Canada.** Here we see one of the few examples in the world of a long-standing residents panel advising a municipal government. The Toronto Planning Review Panel, run by MASS LBP ("MASS Led by People"), provides a representative, community-centric voice to the city's planning division, complementing the work of other advisory bodies. It is made up of thirty-two randomly selected residents from across Toronto who meet regularly over the course of two years. Since its creation in 2015, the TPRP has influenced dozens of projects of strategic city-wide importance and is rapidly becoming an important part of the city's planning, design, policies, and projects.

We invite you to imagine the sort of intractable issues that might be tackled in your home city or country. If you are reading this in the United States, for instance, deliberative democracy might provide a means to discuss the pros and cons of amending the constitution to reform the electoral college. It might debate gun control laws or environmental standards. Or it might help a city decide the best way to police its streets or manage gentrification.

Citizens' assemblies and other forms of deliberative mini-publics are not a magical cure for all that ails a contemporary democracy. Well-organized deliberation, however, engages ordinary citizens in an unbiased, comprehensive dialogue. This engagement is an antidote to cynicism and political resentment—and in today's polarized world, it may provide an answer to populism and the accompanying growing distrust of elites, which has been especially poisonous in the body politic. Imagine demonstrating a different possibility, however. Imagine a political system that brings citizens into the room and allows them the space, time, and supports to deliberate and produce recommendations. Imagine the elite listening to those voices, and the trust resulting from being seen to do so.

In Ireland, we were fortunate to see this imagined future become a reality. In the next part of this essay, we will discuss the fundamentals of making it a reality in other democracies, too.

:::::::::::
:::::::::::
:::::::::::

Part II

Designing a Citizens' Assembly

Across established democracies like Ireland, although electoral participation is generally declining, participation is expanding into new forms of action. Today, more people are signing petitions, joining citizen interest groups, and engaging in unconventional forms of political action. The large expansion of these public interest groups, social movements, and NGOs has made new opportunities for people to get more directly involved in the political system. To put it another way, we're starting to see a departure from the traditional form of democracy that was vote-centered— one in which the citizen's role was passive, essentially being asked once every few years to decide on whether to "vote the rascals out." The new form of democracy is increasingly voice-centered, with more active citizens engaging more critically between elections.[21] People who might not vote, for instance, will take part in a demonstration against the closure of a local hospital or lobby their politicians for increased school funding. This voice-centered involvement is where citizens' assemblies can contribute most, by providing an appropriate forum for engagement and ensuring that any such engagement, if critical, is also constructive.

How can we make the most of this power, if we are to harness it? Citizens' assemblies can make an important contribution to our system of representative democracy, but foremost, they need to be established for a purpose. What is it there to do? In other words, what is the assembly's agenda? In most cases, the agenda is set by the government that has established it, though in East Belgium and Madrid (discussed in part I), the assembly might set its own agenda. It need not be a national government that establishes a citizens' assembly, of course: it could be established by a local government authority, by a planning body, by an interest group seeking to promote a certain agenda, or—as in the Brexit example—by academics seeking to demonstrate the benefits of such an approach. In the discussion below, however, we are assuming that the citizens' assembly is being established by a government— as was the case in Ireland.

Another consideration is cost—how expensive is a well-run process? Unfortunately, context matters: some things cost more in certain countries than others (e.g. the cost of the venue, the price an expert commands, or the distance members need to travel). So does the assembly's scope: the price tag expands with the calendar. But, in general, an assembly not be prohibitively expensive. Each Irish process cost little more than 1 million euros[22]—and given that each one of these operated for more than a year, the people in Ireland got pretty good value for their money, considering the important policy outcomes that resulted.

The Irish cases of deliberative democracy show how citizens' assemblies can move the needle of public sentiment, guide the minds of the political elite, and allay citizen cynicism in politics and democracy, particularly in a moment of crisis. But for these benefits to be realized, and for the time and cost of creating such a body, it is imperative that a citizens' assembly is well-designed. A badly run deliberative process—one whose members are not selected truly at random or where biased evidence is introduced as neutral—could wreak havoc. Poorly designed processes will only alienate citizens from politics even more and further damage trust. We thus need to think carefully about how we design public participation.

There are six core features of a citizens' assembly:

1. the process by which members are selected;
2. the process's organization and leadership;
3. how these members are informed and educated about the issues;
4. how members discuss these issues;

5. engagement with the wider public; and
6. how the citizens' assemblies recommendations are dealt with.

Feature 1: Randomly Chosen Members

As a deliberative mini-public, a citizens' assembly requires its members to be chosen by random selection. This addresses two important aspects of the process. First, ordinary, regular citizens should be the ones involved—citizens selected not on the basis of who they are or what they might know, but rather simply because they hold a true mirror up to society (i.e., the group should reflect good "descriptive representation"). Random selection ensures that the wider public understands people just like them are deliberating, that their voices will be listened to, and that ordinary people—and not special interest groups—are driving policy.

And, second, the citizens should be selected, not elected: they are not there to represent certain sectors or interests. They should not receive a "mandate" by virtue of having run for office or led a cause. Their membership should be the sole result of being chosen in a lottery.

This process of random selection—or "sortition"—results in a very particular atmosphere in a citizens' assembly; very different, for instance, from the experience of the 2011 Icelandic Constitutional Council, whose twenty-five citizen-members were elected. Having "run for office," they felt that they had a mandate to represent the views of their electors—and this attitude tends to encourage a sense of starting from fixed positions. By contrast, in a citizens' assembly, the members see themselves as selected for the task of engaging in open, constructive debate, and that they should be open to the possibility that their positions might change.

There are different ways in which the random selection might occur. But—across the world—mini-publics for the most part operate under the principle that the process is not "pure" random selection: to do so with such relatively small numbers (ninety-nine members in the Irish case) runs the risk of certain demographics being underrepresented. To avoid that risk, the selection method is stratified random selection. In Ireland, there were a series of quotas (sex, age, socioeconomic status, and region) that had to be filled.[23] A polling company, RED C, won the contract to carry out the recruitment process. Sampling from the voting lists for presidential elections or electoral register, their method was to go door to door until they had selected ninety-nine citizens to fill the quotas set out in table 1.

It is important that the members are well looked after—in return for giving up their valuable time. Their travel costs should be covered; the accommodation and food should be of a reasonable standard; childcare and spousal supports should be provided (to ensure that young mothers are not

Table 1: Key demographic targets for selecting members of the Irish Citizens' Assembly, 2016–2018

Target groups		Number of members
Sex	Male	48
	Female	51
Age	18–24	10
	25–39	29
	40–54	28
	55+	32
Socioeconomic status	Middle to upper-middle class	45
	Lower-middle to working class	48
	Farming community	6
Region	Dublin	28
	Rest of Leinster	25
	Munster	27
	Connacht/Ulster	19
Total		99

Note: Targets based on Central Statistics Office data.
Source: RED C, an Irish provider of research-based consultancy services

excluded from the process); and they should receive an appropriate honorarium (a small fee—which could be as little as $100 a day) in recompense. The Canadian and Dutch citizens' assemblies managed this better than the Irish ones (e.g., no honorarium was provided in the Irish cases), which resulted in virtually no turnover of members in the former cases, compared to quite high turnover in the latter.

Feature 2: Effective Leadership

From the outset, a citizens' assembly needs a leadership structure that ensures fairness but doesn't stifle the bottom-up nature of a good mini-public. Discussions need to be run professionally, transparently, and inclusively, which—we've found—are the product of three layers of guidance.

In the first is a top leadership group—in the Irish process, this was called "the secretariat." This group was in charge of the process: ensuring that the government's objectives for the process were met, dealing with the nuts and bolts of running the assembly day by day, and managing both the internal and external faces of the operation. Pragmatically, this means having an independent and respected chair (e.g., in our convention a highly prominent former charity chief, and in the assembly, a senior member of the judiciary) as well as a professional secretariat. In the Irish case, this comprised a senior civil servant, on hiatus from other duties, supported by a small team of civil servants, also on leave from other duties, and other professionals with press and social media experience. In the Canadian cases, the secretariat was established as a separate entity from the civil service, which arguably gave it a greater degree of independence from the government.

The second crucial layer of guidance is an expert advisory group. These are experts who are judged to be independent and objective on the matters at hand. For instance, when our assembly was dealing with abortion, the group's membership consisted of a mix of legal experts, medics and ethicists; when the topic switched to climate change, then a different mix of experts comprised the advisory group. In all cases, its role is to ensure that the experts who speak to the citizen members provide rigorous, accurate information. The group's key responsibilities include finding suitable experts, briefing them, and communicating with them about the content of the briefing documents: these documents are circulated to all assembly members several days before. This group also works with the secretariat to train and educate; this crucial part of the deliberative process is designed to bring all the members up to speed on the topic they are discussing. In this role, the group tracks how discussions unfold and helps advise on the issues. We can't stress enough how important the experts are. It's their information that will be debated, and it may form the basis for the assembly's final recommendations.

Third and finally is the citizen leadership. As a deliberative process, citizen members need to have a significant voice of their own. While inevitably there is an element of top-down management, not least to ensure that major objectives are met and the process moves along on schedule, it is important that members feel a sense of ownership. To that end, one of the first acts of a citizens' assembly should be the establishment of a small steering group elected from among the members: in the Irish cases this was done at the end of the first weekend of deliberation. Their role is to represent the interests of the wider membership, meet with the secretariat and the expert advisory group, react to the proposed agenda for each meeting, and make their own suggestions on how best to proceed. For instance, midway through the Citizens' Assembly's discussions on abortion, the steering group requested and received an extra weekend to discuss the issue.

Feature 3: Informed Discussions

By virtue of the selection process, citizen members start with a low information base. It is the fact that these are ordinary citizens who might know very little about the subject matter that attracts the most criticism—the point commonly made is that these citizens lack the capacity or experience to discuss complex matters.

The problem with such criticisms is that they tend to conflate two things. It is undoubtedly true that regular citizens are unlikely to have much prior expertise with the issue they've been asked to discuss, but—as countless studies in the academic field have shown—they most certainly have the capacity.

Informed deliberation is impossible unless members receive suitable expertise, which commonly comes from the short, written briefing documents provided by subject-matter experts. Such experts also appear as witnesses who are available to answer questions, and the assembly's leadership should ensure that there is sufficient time for members to hear and deliberate among themselves on the experts' information.

In short, the inclusion of experts is crucial to this process, but they are included for their expertise; they are not members of the assembly. Additionally, depending on the topic, the voices of organized interests (advocates, NGOs, and any other parties that have an interest in the topic being discussed) might also be helpful. These presentations require an allotment of time in the schedule, as well as a clear caveat to the members that these are not the voices of independent experts.

When and for how long the experts are included in the process is time-dependent. The approach adopted in the Canadian and Dutch cases was to have a "learning" or "boot-camp" stage for the first couple of meetings, in which the members would receive reading material and hear from experts, with the aim being that members would emerge with enough expertise for informed discussion. A similar approach was adopted in the Irish Citizens' Assembly when it discussed abortion: across the five weekends, the members were given plenty of opportunity to develop their knowledge base so as to feel confident discussing the issue.

Not all assemblies will have the luxury of five weekends or more. What if you only have just one weekend or even less? This requires a broad-brush approach to bringing members up to the speed on the issues being discussed. Where a training boot camp is impossible, the alternative strategy is to use the available time judiciously—using the experts to provide members with information on key points, the range of alternatives that are available, and a sense of the likely consequences that would flow from their decision.

Here is one example of a two-weekend discussion, the convention's debate on Ireland's electoral system. Experts focused on introducing the members to the different electoral systems in use. (Their clever example had members use different electoral systems to select menu options for dinner and then demonstrated how the various outcomes were heavily influenced by the electoral system that was used.) The experts also outlined the key values that underlay a certain choice of electoral system, and they reviewed key outcomes from different systems, e.g., the representation of women in parliament, the choice available to voters on the ballot paper, and so forth. It was also made clear to the members that they were not expected to come up with a detailed design for an electoral system, but that instead they should simply consider what type of electoral system they would prefer, overall.

Feature 4: High-Quality Deliberation

The fourth key ingredient to a good mini-public is the use of deliberative techniques that ensure a calm, reflective, informed, open discussion. This requires an emphasis on small roundtable deliberation. To ensure this, it is important that the membership formally agree to certain rules and procedures relating (among other things) to fairness, equality of voice, being open to the other side's views, etc. If time allows, consider having the membership draw up these rules themselves. At the very least, however, a discussion at the start of the citizens' assembly should set these guidelines; and they should be regularly reiterated during the process.

The other important ingredient to high-quality deliberation is the use of trained facilitators at each table whose primary role is to ensure that the discussion meets the objectives (i.e., calm, reflective, informed, and open) and that each member has equal voice.

Besides the training, debriefing, and monitoring of facilitators, our experience also reinforces the value of asking the members in regular surveys what they felt about the process. These surveys ensured a strong element of quality control of the process—the leadership received these feedback reports after each meeting, and in turn shared them with the members.

Among other things, our survey was interested in measuring the deliberative quality of the roundtable discussions over the course of the five weekends focused on abortion. The intensity of those discussions provides a hard test of the deliberative process's success. We found that the levels of satisfaction remained high across these five weekends, as they did across all eleven weekends of discussion: most members felt that they were free to raise their views, that they had ample speaking opportunities, and that other members respected what they had to say. Specifically, we received a total of between seventy-six and ninety-one responses out of ninety-nine possible members (because attendance fluctuated over the five weeks). The survey asked respondents to rate their satisfaction with aspects of the process on a scale of 1 (strongly disagree) to 5 (strongly agree). They responded with strong agreement to statements including, "Members respected my say," and, "I had ample speaking opportunities." They responded with strong disagreement to the statement, "I didn't feel free to raise my views." Members were somewhat more equivocal in their responses to the statement, "Some members dominated the discussion," a trend that wavered between neutrality and mild disagreement over the five weeks.

Interviews with a sample of the Citizens' Assembly members in the final weeks of its operation also reveal high levels of satisfaction with the process. As one member put it, "The beauty of the whole thing [is] it's a neutral environment. There's a great level of respect for everybody's opinions: we haven't had any fisticuffs. There have been strong views expressed at times, but nobody's fallen out over it." Similar views were expressed by another member. "Everyone could make their point.... There was no shouting: [if anyone tried to take over] they were put in their place.... I felt I could ask anything and didn't feel I would be shouted down by anyone at the table." There was general agreement, however, that matters were more tense during the discussions on abortion than for any of the other topics.

Feature 5: Engagement with the Wider Public

By its nature, a citizens' assembly is a mini-public. It is important that it does not ignore the "maxi-public"—those other citizens outside the room who may or may not be looking in with varying degrees of interest and knowledge about the assembly's work.

A transparent process reassures the public that their peers are looking at the best available evidence, questioning experts thoroughly, and making carefully considered decisions. A key organizational feature of a well-run deliberative process is that it should be fully transparent: there should be no basis for any criticism of it seeking to hide details from wider members of the public.

This principle ensures equality of access for those outside of the process. This was something that was stressed in all the Irish processes—an emphasis on openness, on the need to operate with as much transparency as possible. In our case, all plenary sessions were broadcast live on the website, though the roundtable discussions were kept private. Submissions on each topic by members of the public and interest groups were published on the website. Ultimately, the livestreaming of plenary sessions attracted a large number of viewers, both in Ireland and abroad.

Time should be set aside in the schedule for "backyard conversations" with the wider public. In the Canadian cases, for instance, the members were involved in town hall meetings with other citizens from their area. This provides a useful feedback mechanism for the membership, a reality check on the topic being considered and on the recommendations that the members might be contemplating.

Feature 6: Responding to the Citizens' Assembly

Now the citizens' assembly has finished its work. It has made its careful recommendations. Members go home feeling proud of the effort they've made and their role in their nation's democracy. Something good has been accomplished—or has it? Will their work languish, or will the government take it seriously?

The final issue is how to deal with the output of a citizens' assembly. There are some who argue that an assembly's recommendations should be binding when, for instance, a recommendation is supported by most members. We disagree. Based on our opening position that a citizens' assembly is there to *support* our existing system of democracy, it makes more sense for its recommendations to be advisory rather than binding. They should feed back into the wider political system, either in the form of a referendum or political debate in the relevant representative institution (parliament, congress, etc.). The risk, of course, is that the sponsor of the citizens' assembly might ignore inconvenient recommendations, cherry-picking the more palatable ones and ignoring the rest. To minimize this risk, we suggest that in the design stage, leaders should craft clear guidelines on how the assembly's recommendations will be dealt with, and these guidelines should be treated as a plan. As we discussed earlier, politicians' early sense of investment in the process can improve their follow-through after the assembly concludes. So will steady, widespread public awareness of the process. Democracy can only evolve for the better if important decisions remain in the public eye and politicians are made to represent their constituents' carefully reasoned views.

Conclusion
Looking to the Future

People have started to expect more from democracy than just the opportunity to vote for a party every few years. Participation is growing: not just in signing petitions (see the six million who signed a Brexit petition, for example) but also in social movements, NGOs, and other sorties. These trends suggest that there is public appetite to be more involved and to narrow the representation gap. Rising public cynicism and declining public trust suggests that such involvement is critical.

The point is that citizen assemblies and other deliberative institutions can strengthen representative democracy. Restoring public trust requires several factors. First, citizens must feel that their voice matters; the answer to this is creating deliberative mini-publics in which the government is invested. The process itself builds trust in the political process and helps narrow the political legitimacy gap. And of course it produces that same evidence which can then be used within the debate and for debunking and fact-checking by media in later reporting. Second, citizens need to regain trust in each other. The answer is a transparent process staffed by experts so that we can stop reaching for cynical, factually untrue cliché[3] about the ineptitude of ordinary citizens. Third, democracy should continue to grow and evolve. One answer is in testing out ways to make deliberative mini-publics a permanent part of the political structure, such as is being tested in places like East Belgium and Madrid. A democracy that is experimenting and evolving is—we suggest—one that is less likely to be prone to severe crisis.

We would like to encourage policymakers and governments to think hard about ways to truly listen to citizen voices—to design participatory processes that are representative, inclusive, deliberative, free from manipulation, informed, and influential. Otherwise, politicians and policymakers are left to rely on the work of special interest groups and opinion polls to generalize the public's views. These methods are, however, almost by definition "top of the head" representations. For complicated issues that require complex background information and open minds rather than rigid views, pollsters and lobbies tell us too little. Deliberation provides a far richer account of citizen preferences, viewpoints, and visions for their future.

Our vision is of democracies that incorporate everyday people into major public decisions, especially those that present democratic structures struggle to address.[24] We have seen how a meaningful democracy is not just possible, but eminently practical and achievable.

Acknowledgments

This essay tells the story of a journey we've been taking together over the best part of a decade. We are very grateful to Sarah Cypher, who has helped us to write this in a more user-friendly format—it has been a pleasure to work with you. We wish to acknowledge and thank our various collaborators who have joined us at different stages on this journey. Our We the Citizens project was done in collaboration with Elaine Byrne, Órla de Burca, Caroline Erskine, Úna Faulkner, Fiach Mac Conghail, and Eoin O'Malley. During the work of the Convention on the Constitution, we had the good fortune of working together on the academic and legal team with Clodagh Harris, Lia O'Hegarty, and Eoin O'Malley; and we benefited from the access we were given to the process by the chair, Tom Arnold, and the secretary, Art O'Leary. Our engagement with the Irish Citizens'

Assembly was supported by a grant awarded to us by the Irish Research Council and the Secretariat of the Irish Citizens' Assembly; and our access to the CA was facilitated by the chair, Mary Laffoy; the secretary, Sharon Finegan; her colleague, Gráinne Hynes; and the rest of their team. Finally, we acknowledge the hard work and commitment of over three hundred Irish citizens who gave up their valuable time to engage in one of these three mini-publics—these are the deliberative heroes of this piece!

Notes

1 Jane Suiter, "A Constitutional Moment: Taking Advantage of a Confluence of Events," in *Foundation Stone: Notes Towards a Constitution for a 21st-Century Republic*, ed. Theo Dorgan (Dublin: New Island, 2013), 469–483.

2 For a contemporary account of the crisis and its severity, see Niamh Hardiman, ed., *Irish Governance in Crisis* (Manchester: Manchester University Press, 2012).

3 Michael Marsh, David Farrell, and Gail McElroy, eds. *A Conservative Revolution? Electoral Change in Twenty-First Century Ireland* (Oxford: Oxford University Press, 2017).

4 Min Reuchamps and Jane Suiter, eds. *Constitutional Deliberative Democracy in Europe* (Colchester, Essex: ECPR Press, 2016).

5 Peter Mair, *Ruling the Void: The Hollowing-Out of Western Democracy* (London: Pluto Press, 2013).

6 Patrick Fournier, Henk van der Kolk, Kenneth Carty, André lais, and Jonathan Rose, eds. *When Citizens Decide: Lessons from*

Citizen Assemblies on Electoral Reform (Oxford: Oxford University Press, 2011).

7 See David Farrell and Peter Stone, "Sortition and Mini-Publics: A Different Kind of Representation," in *Handbook of Political Representation*, ed. Robert Rohrschneider and Jacques Thomassen (Oxford: Oxford University Press, forthcoming).

8 They also served as a useful means for us to learn how to do this in practice, ensuring that by the time we reached our second phase—the Citizens' Assembly—we were confident about how to implement our own deliberative process in practice.

9 James Bohman and William Rehg, *Deliberative Democracy: Essays on Reason and Politics* (Boston: MIT Press, 1997), 321; and Amy Gutmann and Dennis Thompson, *Why Deliberative Democracy?* (Princeton, NJ: Princeton University Press, 2004), 7.

10 For details on the academic project underlying this initiative, and our key findings, see: David Farrell, Eoin O'Malley, and Jane Suiter, "Deliberative Democracy in Action Irish-Style: The 2011 *We the Citizens* Pilot Citizens' Assembly," *Irish Political Studies* 28 (2013): 99–113; Jane Suiter, David Farrell, and Eoin O'Malley, "When Do Deliberative Citizens Change Their Opinions? Evidence from an Irish Citizens' Assembly," *International Political Science Review* 37 (2016): 198–212; and Eoin O'Malley, David Farrell, and Jane Suiter, "Does Talking Matter? A Quasi-Experiment Assessing the Impact of Deliberation and Information on Opinion Change," *International Political Science Review* (2019): online first.

11 For high-profile deliberative mini-publics of this type, the choice of chair is critical. In this instance, Arnold was highly respected most particularly for his work as the director of one of Ireland's leading charities. In the subsequent Irish Citizens' Assembly, the chair, Mary Laffoy, was a supreme court judge. Similarly in the Canadian and Dutch citizens' assemblies, the

chairs were highly regarded individuals (i.e., a former university president, a former judge, and a well-known columnist and television host).

12 For details on the Convention on the Constitution, see: Jane Suiter, David Farrell, and Clodagh Harris, "The Irish Constitutional Convention: A Case of 'High Legitimacy?,' " in *Constitutional Deliberative Democracy in Europe*, ed. M. Reuchamps and J. Suiter (Colchester, Essex: ECPR Press, 2016).

13 More details are provided in Tom Arnold, David Farrell, and Jane Suiter, "Lessons from a Hybrid Sortition Chamber: The 2012–14 Irish Constitutional Convention," in *Legislature by Lot: Transformative Designs for Deliberative Governance*, ed. John Gastil and Erik Olin Wright (London: Verso, 2019).

14 See the documentary streamed on Netflix called *The 34th: The Story of Marriage Equality,* directed by Linda Cullen and Vanessa Gildea (https://ifi.ie/the-34th).

15 David Farrell, Jane Suiter, Clodagh Harris, and Kevin Cunningham, "The Effects of Mixed Membership in a Deliberative Forum: The Irish Constitutional Convention of 2012–14," *Political Studies* (2019): online first.

16 Ronan McGreevy, "Oireachtas Given a Mandate to Change the Eighth Amendment," *Irish Times*, April 24, 2017.

17 Leah McDonald, "Citizens' Assembly: 64% Want Abortion without Restriction," *Irish Daily Mail*, April 24, 2017.

18 "Putting It Up to the Politicians," *Irish Times*, April 25, 2017.

19 For more on the Citizens' Assembly, see David Farrell, Jane Suiter, and Clodagh Harris, " 'Systematizing' Constitutional Deliberation: The 2016–18 Citizens' Assembly in Ireland," *Irish Political Studies* (2018): online first.

20 John Dryzek, André Bächtiger, Simone Chambers, Joshua Cohen, James Druckman, Andrea Felicetti, James Fishkin, David

Farrell, Archon Fung, Amy Gutmann, Hélène Landemore, Jane Mansbridge, Sofie Marien, Michael Neblo, Simon Niemeyer, Maija Setälä, Rune Slothuus, Jane Suiter, Dennis Thompson, and Mark E. Warren, "The Crisis of Democracy and the Science of Deliberation," *Science* 363 (March 2019): 1144–1146.

21 David Farrell, "'Stripped Down' or Reconfigured Democracy," *West European Politics* 37 (2014): 439–455.

22 Information provided by the secretariats.

23 Here we describe the recruitment process for the 2016–2018 Irish Citizens' Assembly; we followed the same procedure as applied in the 2012–2014 Convention on the Constitution.

24 Also see Democracy R&D, an international network of scholars and practitioners that seeks to help decision makers "take hard decisions and build public trust" (www.democracyrd.org). This is an excellent first stop for anyone seeking advice for implementing a deliberative mini-public in their area.

About the Authors

David M. Farrell is a Full Professor of Politics at University College Dublin, where he is head of the School of Politics and International Relations. He is a member of the Royal Irish Academy, and an executive committee member of the European Consortium for Political Research. His research is centered on how contemporary democracies operate, with particular focus on the themes of political representation, political parties, elections, and—over the last decade—deliberative democracy.

Jane Suiter is an Associate Professor in the School of Communications at Dublin City University and Director of the Institute for Future Media and Journalism, also at DCU. She serves on the Standing Committee of the ECPR standing group on Democratic Innovations, and the Social Science Committee of the Royal Irish Academy. She is also the PI of two European Union H2020 projects. Her expertise lies mainly in the area of the public sphere; in particular, (dis)information, participation and political engagement, focusing on deliberative democracy and citizens' assemblies.

Lightning Source UK Ltd.
Milton Keynes UK
UKHW041509101119
353247UK00010B/29/P